Words
and
Consequence

by

K.M.F

For my brother, who inspired this.

Contents:

INTRODUCTION: THE WILL OF THE AUTHOR 1

CHAPTER 1: OF WATER AND WORDS 3

CHAPTER 2: THE REALITY OF WORDS: THE LIE AND THE TRUTH 9

CHAPTER 3: HOW TO VOICE OUR WILL/ THE INDIVIDUALITY OF
WORDS 15

CHAPTER 4: CONVERSATION AND CULTURE 21

CHAPTER 5: VIOLENT MEANINGLESS WORDS 28

CHAPTER 6: THE BEGINNING OF MY THOUGHTS ABOUT HOPE 34

CHAPTER 7: WORDS AND THIS WORLD 37

CHAPTER 8: HOW TO SPOT FRIENDSHIP IN WORDS 44

CHAPTER 9: LOVE, LIFE, AND CHOICE 50

CHAPTER 10: WORDS AS RELAXATION 57

CHAPTER 11: FIGHTING A BLEEDING BATTLE 64

CHAPTER 12: THE END OF WORDS/ HOW TO END WORDS 71

Introduction

The Will Of The Author

I never wanted to be a writer. There are so many other things at which I excel that I could do in life and go far but writing is the one thing I do well with the least amount of effort. In fact, it is the reason why I was created on this Earth, to write for the people and to change their lives with the weight of my words. I started writing to explain the things that happened in my life that terrified me and the endless movements I have endured to become someone. My will has not always been my choice in fact I was forced into what I am today because of the danger and difficulty of this world. At every turn was a test seeking to tear into ashes every part that was a piece of the real me. The will of the author should not be wrought from a reaction to stimuli but from a deeper part of within that is seeking to change one thing for the better. Be that a person, situation, or straight inconvenience an author's will has got to come from what they want to inflict, and not the will of the people. I have grown tired of hearing from teacher after teacher that the authors will and intent is the inherent property of the reader. Let me enlighten you, sweetheart. It's not! My will, my words, my way is the direction the story will take. Be it random loops of infinite thought or sonorous melodies of syllables; I will not have my will stolen at every turn, to be expended at the purpose of profit, resulting in the shrewdness of creativity. I am who I am! The author, the storyteller, the bard with the power to sink ships, launch hearts and broker time. Thus, is the lengths and edges of my will, the inherent power within. The first thing gifted to man by Heaven was free will and with it the ability to take leaps of faith, flying into the depths of the unknown in order to reach a profession of progress. So, I say, take flight my will, become what you are not and embrace the tale of one called Author. Because I never wanted to be a writer.

Chapter 1

Of Water and Words

The Written Word: It may not seem like the most obvious thing, but water has leaked itself into the depths of our words and was absorbed by way of meaning. When I refer to water and its relation to words it can take on many definitions in writing. Water has three forms, solid (ice), liquid (droplets), and gas (steam) which are brought out by our emotions tempered into the steel of letters. When writing about water, a person can choose any of its forms and exercise that voice into any style of writing be it poetry, prose, or the traditional letter. I often wonder though what water means in general, like what emotion does it portray when put into words. Is it sadness, joy, triumph, splendor, majesty? Or is it the darkest shifts of a soul's inner monologue resulting in inked pages of death, destitution, and ebonic bones of coal? I have written many things in the burst of a moment of emotion that was significant but simply held no meaning, only reaching the pursuit of something more.

If anything, when you are drowning in words too bitter to say, you can only say water. Well, what does that mean? Is water just an anagram for the truth that is hidden so greatly down that the only word you can use to describe it is water? Yes, water. That glowing aqua, iridescent blue banished into the descent of letters that simply no one knows but the inner persona of one's self. Or is water in some ways like a poison? A necessary bitter concoction that once taken in can never be replaced or replenished resulting in a numbingly lackluster composite shell of reality. You see, water is an instrument framed by the masterfulness of the wandering bard who tames it to an eerie perfection that is acceptable in the eyes of society. Water is the outcast who haunts the painted halls, searching, no seeking, for the bays of acknowledgment, asking but receiving none. Water is the savior in the treble of the oasis that saves the straggling wanderer lying parched on sand throne.

You cannot tell me; water is not a living thing, an essence that once given rise to falls in a cascading line of waves that seeks out the minds of the affected and inflicts a strange sort of awareness upon its parishioners, who will never be the same. The essence of water is the shell that traps it inside seeking to bury it within the expression of a ship, never to be seen by the light of humanity. Thus, is the expression, thus is water; the strange creativity sparked from the jagged lines of humble cannibals whose heads became frustrated by the languidness of the struggle that it is to live in this world. We are all like the water, straining to live in a sea of folk that is both solid, liquid, and gas. Be it ice, snow, vapor, or the perilousness of a rushing river; water is upon us all. It shall not be taken for naught! So, when I speak of the correlation between water and words, I am penning out the remarks that make water what it is.

For the Master of Water is God who created it for the throng of humanity to survive off. If I am not making this clear, water is like the sawmill powered by the sheer force of the tiniest of streams, baked into the hulls of great galleons. Water is in everything, be it the driest roots of pine bark or in the thirstiest strands of leaves competing for the one drop that ensures survival. So, water is survival, the greater struggle to become the top line, the one who lives is determined by the will of the water and the blessing of the one true God. So, I say let us write of water and words, and let this emotion find itself in all incessant works of literature that are sure to come in this dying age. For water is also like the age, that traces lines of descent from one mode of time to the next, but the immense question is does water age? Heck does water feel. Is it not the mind of the people to question these questionable ideas and bring forth some sort of suitable answer? Tell me the truth about water. Speak it, set it free, and tell the world of water and words.

On the other hand, perhaps water is a sacred blue fire that seeks to never have an end spreading from one cloud to the next, oh wait dont scientists call this the cycle of water? If water were to have a cycle, you are essentially arguing that we all have cycles since we are water as well. But should we limit ourselves to the half-written theory that is the cycle of water or choose to believe in the humble imperfections that are the musings of humanity, elected to create a single veritable human understanding. So, although we just accept this cycle of water, can we not just believe in the writing of water and words as well? But water is to not just be weaved into the throws of human expression of melodies of sweet words, but evident in the watery water that which we speak it as well.

The Spoken Word/ The way of Water:

As we speak, there is this high energy we possess that fuels the fire that is the strength of our words. It is water, flooding over cheeks of grainy skin, pumping our tongues to do the powerful work that is speaking. For water even correlates with speaking as we have established water as an emotion present to the benefit of our words. So, tell me, when you speak does the feeling of water have anything to do with those words? Water can be expressed in any variety of ways and can it be sold as sadness, anger, and the spirit of life? Your words are like water as it flows from the feet of stepless mountains unrestrained by the artificial creations of man. As you know, speech comes from God and is accredited to his likeness, so when you speak, say all with the cleanliness of water that is pure in its clear and aspiring way.

Do not say, with the resonating tones of the rainfall storm, but instead be honest with the way you place your words. As water condenses into the dew that scatters the Earth, you must speak with the gentility that matures from the hard work of torrenting rain. For whether we speak with the idyllic beauty of water drops cascading down the river stream or with the passive-aggressiveness that is the summer monsoon, we must control our words to be used to the best effect possible. Do not use the words of water to inflict the seed of personal vengeance, weaponized in a stream of lies and faux paus, that seek to break the branches of the rock that is the human heart. For words like the water have the potential to rip apart and erode layers of rock, breaking piece by piece at a time, until all that is left are shards to be roughly shoved together again by some manmade machine that can never replace the grandeur that is the water of one's real self.

The water of words can be put to an opposing effect by throwing down and away the shields of our scars that have been patched together by the rough manmade machine. So, let's patch it together and see if it works is the new motto of writers everywhere and let me tell you! It does not work that way! If you want your words to flow like the precipice of sweet dripping honey, do not treat your words as if they mean nothing. Give value to them, bring forth great meaning from them, and make every effort to discover new ones. For words like water are a discovery, just waiting to be spoken anew, breathed by every generation that changes the discourse of history by coming alive! The veritable fashion today must be done away with, and it is your destiny to take a word and boil it until it takes on the shadows of a new form and then let it burst forth from you like a dam because that is the job of a writer. When tying together water and words, your job is not to be the common carnival monkey who runs through the streets rampantly but to be organized and straight moving like the placid surface of a lake. Because it takes words to have water and water to have words, and we must not confuse the map that distinguishes them as separate, distinct entities working on voicing the will of all.

Chapter 2

The Reality of Words:

The lie and the Truth

The Distrustful reality of words:

When looking at the human condition, I have found that we all have told lies. Written them, said them, spoken them in the distance, whatever form we try to excuse them as they are all lies. I'm here to tell you that these words we have given out as the great assurance, a way of covering up our sins, or just as a casual answer to end an uncomfortable situation are just that a convenient answer to all of life's problems. I am not accusing anyone of what I have not done myself. I have told all kinds of lies to cover up the messes that I could not be responsible for that I was not willing to be responsible for. I just shoved them upon the next waiting person who I thought could do better than me with them.

Thus, it is the essence of a lie, that syllable we echo onto others to avoid the most real problems in our worlds. And now even the lie that made up the unknowable secret parts of one's own life has become the world; it has become the news. Oh yes, the fake news that boldly states. "This man died today". We all know it is not the truth, yet we are so quick to kill the innocent with our lies that we never stop to consider the consequence of our words. For example, how about the family who experiences the news that their child, the innocent one has died and is devastated at the reality they now face. A well-placed black lie made out to be some sort of truth spreads the news of the death of a beloved person and crushes every hope, dream and life-long wish that has been written into the soul of what one family felt for that person.

Imagine if that was what all fake news and propaganda was, the soul-crushing wind of paper that flew to the doors of one who just wanted to live without hearing that he was dead. And as that ghost of a person comes home to a house filled with the shattered cries of his dream, then you will see the ultimate consequence of the lie. Be it written, spoken, whatever crazy excuse you try to call it, do not lie with words. Instead tell the bloody truth, expose the lie that threatens to destroy a family in this world, and face the reality that means being responsible for our words. When we are responsible and acknowledge the vast imperfections in ourselves, we can see a great change in the human condition. As humans, if we continue to tell these blaise, baseless lies, we will continue to create a world for our children, family, and ourselves, a world full of distrustful words.

We might as well call the world a lie because we are not living up to the potential of our truth. Fire comes from our hearts when we drop everything to speak the hardest steps that we have taken to ensure something is not told. That evil will never be uprooted and brought to the surface to be defeated by the white knight if we do not tell our truth. Tell the truth! Tell the truth, my friends; it will change your life. Like the truthful word that we are all imperfect people, and we need not spread any more lies to shield us from the blame of what it is really like to experience this world. If you tell the truth and refuse the distrustful reality of words, mountains will move for you, and I promise you that it's not a death sentence but the key to a higher form of living; such is the value of truth.

Part 2: The Value of Truth

The value of truth is a very interesting concept indeed, and many think that words of truth can have the most powerful impact. If you think that not telling lies is amazing enough, what about the truthful notes of the syllable of ourselves. In fact, what is truth in word exactly? Truth, to me seems to be a lifelong pursuit of passionate answers found in the harrowed walls of the cave of silence. Even then truth seems to be some sort of mysticism, enchanting the eyes of others, drawing them deeper in as it is spoken aloud. When we examine truth in words, there is one thing that as people we seem to forget, and that is the importance of truth.

When speaking to our friends, there may come times when we have to dance on our precipices and expose the real truth of how we feel about them, even if it seems wrong to speak to them in such a cruel way. Our friends may not expect the truth, but it's always better in the end, to be honest when interacting with others. The kind of truth we tell takes on a personality of its own because it is the tone of voice we use that controls how others see what we say. The truth can be dark and unrelenting like the thundering tone of a shouting voice, or it can be like a gentle vacant whisper whose lended wing fly's forward to point them in a new direction.

It is easy to believe that truth is one thing when the truth is different to us all. Truth does not care about personal obligation or feeling, even timing; it will be told eventually. Truth seems to be some sort of inconvenience eh. Let me tell you truth is not blind to love and the best kind of love is truth. Although truth is not patient in the way love is, but it does not envy others and seeks to reap the great conclusion that we are all searching for. I know this is not the news you want to hear about truth, but really truth is so strong! Its power is indefinite and however many lies the devil spits in your ear about the outcome of the situation, you must remember that only you can define your truth. Only you can decide whether your life will be filled with the tender and spontaneous kind of love that words of truth are filled with. If you want honesty, first practice truth for honesty is the buildup of truth on a bridged journey to discover what is really hiding in all our hearts.

I know you wish truth did not have to be so hard and so bitter, that the only kind of truth you would want to spit out is poisonous words of water. Lie! Lie! That is the only thing people seem to say today with their faceless expressions, cowering in silence too afraid to spell the truth. Well, let me spell it out for you! The truth died on a cross for you, the way by sacrificing his soul for you. I do not need to tell you his name, but you should know what truth looks like. Its name is Jesus! A humble servant who dedicated his entire life to others and lived the perfect life without consequence is who we should look to when we decide if we want to tell the truth or not. Think about a man bleeding, hanging with the bitter spikes of cascading thorns embedded in his heart with only his arms crying out for truth. Because truth is sacrifice and we must be willing to sacrifice the innocent and even most prideful part of ourselves, to tell the truth regardless of how much it sinks our reputation in the eyes of others. In the eyes of others, Jesus was a man of others who were willing, to tell the truth in a world where was synonymous with death. The truth of words can only be expressed when we open ourselves up to the possibility that practicing honesty is what we should strive to do as good people. In the end, let us look forward to a world that sets aside fake news and laces every word with the solid expression of truthfulness and the spirit of life. Amen.

Chapter 3

How To Voice Our Will/ The Individuality Of Words

I do not know which is more annoying to voice my words alone or to a group of people. I cannot imagine any greater struggle than there is to voice one's will in their words. From page to the podium, the world's most significant fear is how to express one's individual self through words. As an individual who spends every waking moment alone, I can understand the struggle to voice thoughts using words. It is an awkward and frustrating thing to not just tell the truth but to figure out the best way to say something. I mean do not just say the first thing that comes to mind like pickles because that is kind of silly unless you are ordering pickles. But actually think about how you're going to tell whoever your speaking to the severity of a situation, a simple daily thing, or what you have been hiding for so long that's been bottled up, and you cannot wait any longer.

The first thing to remember is that we all have a voice, an uncertain flow within our body that soars to the front whenever we are passionate about something. The secret to voicing one's will through words are to first find that which makes you unique and to create a passion for yourself that you are willing to drop everything for and yet at the same time abandon in the same movement for the sake of what really matters. Because passion can either last a lifetime or fade with the setting sun, yet the great part about life is that it is your own choice of what to do with such a gift, the gift of life. Create your own voice, make it pure, and truly let it embody the person that you are. Do not be afraid to be influenced by the voices of those who inspire you but be careful not to get caught up in the madness of the next big thing.

The only way to be truly us and lift our own voice out to the people to reach them is that we must not become like the people. By becoming like the people, we destroy every sense of who we are for the sake of money, prestige, fame, whatever it is. Our individual voice is not worth any of that; it should not be bought and cannot be bought. Do not sell yourself to the public for the sake of fame; I tried that once and nearly lost everyone I cared about in the process. Fame is not worth your integrity no matter how shiny a bow is stamped on the price tag that the world is willing to pay for your silence. No truer words have been spoken then is the simple phrase of "Be yourself but don't sell yourself", for these actions will take you far beyond who you originally imagined you were.

When we dare to create our own voice, as individuals, we are not limited to the names people have called us from the beginning. We are not just an identity created by the fickle and few who dare describe who we are trying to become. I believe that the easiest way to voice our own opinion is to find the one thing that we will not give up on no matter what. Be it people, a skill, or the freedom of our own choice, to become who we are is brave. I know the expectation is strong words of encouragement to bring out your inner voice, but I feel that the only way to make you realize yourself is through gentleness. It takes a gentle moment of quiet reflection to see through the mists of one's own life, of the times we failed and of the situations where we failed to say something we wished that could change one person's entire world. So, at this moment, think about how one's life can tell them all they need to say. Because who you are determines your voice of individuality and assures you of who you are.

Part 2: The Plurality of the Voice

Even when we have discovered our individual voices, there is the residual effect of the impact our voices can have on real life. You see as we are born and grow to take on the challenges of life; we will find our own voice measured out among the voices of those around us. And boy do they never shut up! We all want to be heard and say something, even me but I bet you are getting tired of this stupid author constantly writing like she knows it all. Or perhaps does he know it all? Is voice androgynous or are we all just restricted to one gender and tone of voice of which to speak in? I find myself using the vernacular of my home voice, that which I speak to understand my readers and for them to understand me. Anyway, enough about this wordless author and back to the plurality of the voice.

When speaking in groups, there is something that we have all seen before, and that is the want to have something to say. I may be wrong however as there are people who wish to avoid the crowd and surrender their voice to the multitude to protect their light spirits in the face of the majority enemy. But as the Alphas of our lives, when dealing with the multitude, we must set ourselves apart from this faithless world and turn our opinions into something new, which is voicing our own opinions into rooms where there seems to be no place for them. Let me tell you there is always room for your voice beyond the surface of your own relentless hopes to become more than what people have deemed them to be.

The hardest thing is dealing with those voices who seek to tear apart your spirit as the vultures did to the liver of Prometheus as he was punished for speaking his mind.

However, there is an inherent danger when speaking to the multitude because you will find many who do not like what you have to say. In fact, that's the issue with this world as people attempt to create every sort of negative evil from truthful words spoken not to them but for someone who just needs a sliver of hopeful light in their lives to keep them from losing it all. Honestly, nowadays you need privacy. It seems just to speak your most piercing thoughts as they are as shameful as a woman wearing booty shorts. Correction, an immodest imitation of pants cut in half is what your thoughts become in the eyes of others. The world seeks to crush your dream by cutting your voice in half like that lady crushed those shorts with a pair of scissors that cut too deep in order to create some sinful immodesty that is not the truth! How annoying it is to imagine our voices destroyed by the incessant views of ones who gave up their voices a long time ago. No wonder I work alone as a great lesson is that if you do not choose to think for yourself, other people will.

It seems that in every situation people will try to think for you. Hell, even without asking they do that anyway and try to shove you into the majority class without even imagining what it is to be themselves. The plural voice must not be seceded to just give power to one opinion bought by sacks of gold and deep pockets but instead must remain free with the chance to share all the wonderful things of life with others through daily news. As such, not only can sharing one's voice with others be a positive experience but therein also lies the resistance from those who cannot stand the strong voice of individualism in this world.

For me, I remember an incident where the voices of hatred tortured me every time I stepped in the door. Like a force breathing down my back it never seemed to get better until I left to find myself. The truth is that in this world it is a crime somewhat in the eyes of others to dare to be different. As we look to this day, we cannot become obsessed with the habit that makes people happy. If anything, our voice should not be that of another but must be the voice of our own. There will always be sycophants who will hate what you have to say about life, but I encourage you to be the person you were meant to be, not what others expect you to be. Change those who are of the plural voice and hive mindset to unrelenting individuals of a new world that is not subject to the voices of others. We all have our own voice and must always remember who we are and strive to be.

Chapter 4

Conversation and Culture

Part 1: The Conversation

A h yes, those annoying words we must share with our compatriots to get anything done. The noise of conversation, indignant trilling that floods the streets of vagrant minds, struggling to figure out what to say only to find the other person is gone. You see conversation is communication, and in this world of vast technology and of every face glued to a cellphone, I included, there exists a consistent lack of conversation. As we advance as human beings into a technological era filled with only the thoughts swirling in our mind and sent in tiny brackets of yellowish text, we miss the real personal experience that is conversation. I am not just talking about the simple hello, how are you, and goodbye but an actual conversation between two real people searching for something more. Be it casual, intellectual, or sharing the daily news, there is a constant lack of communication everywhere! I mean honestly, are all people shy or something? How hard is it to go up to a person and ask for a conversation on this planet of 7.5 almost 8 billion unique people? Well, it is hard. Even I must admit it is a challenge to strike up a normal conversation with anyone of my age due to having to compete with a piece of scrap metal for their attention. It's utterly ridiculous! Picture going up to a person and asking their name only to be ignored for a metallic facet called the phone. I know I am ranting here, but this phone must be quite the sweet talker for it to overlook the weird stranger waving their hands in a friendly hello right in front of them. It is like hello look up! To be honest, it seems that the phone is a mirror that Narcissus (the person) looks at constantly to check if they're still beautiful. I get phones are awesome, and all but so is a living, breathing individual right in front of you that just wants to have a conversation! Help a person out and talk to them! Who knows that person could turn out to be your new best friend and all you must do is look up and bam, bingo, new friend!

You see the coolest part about conversation is an opportunity to express any opinion no matter how different and radical it is without consequence. Okay so maybe there is a risk in putting yourself out there, but there is also a risk in not having a conversation. If you are lonely and have no friends and refuse to talk to someone, pressure builds up inside until you either get depression or explode quite literally. Also, another thing about not having a conversation is that you miss out on the people who can become important characters in your life. Ever been in a jam or midlife crisis and phoned a friend who helped you get through that situation? Well, conversation is like that! All you must do is phone a friend by putting down the phone and saying some words. Yet there are always people who will not be your friend and in that case, keep walking and look for other options. Remember we are all fighting a battle inside that nobody knows about and thus we should be kind to others always.

The easiest way to start a conversation is to ask for a name. According to Amal Kassir, an international spoken word artist, "The greatest distance between two people is a name". Your name reflects your will and how you want others to see you as well. As we converse, we meet people with all kinds of different names and who speak various languages. The beautiful part about conversation is language because there are so many ways in which to speak. However, if you speak be aware that others can hear you, and sometimes the right thing to do is say nothing. I encourage you to explore conversation and the words used in it as conversation is so essential to who we are as people. Conversation is the glorious bridge of stringed beads that connects us in a way that only others can understand. The way to move forward is to first stop, look up, and find a conversation. It may even find you if you are lucky.

Part 2: Culture

Culture the one thing that makes up our background and seeks to define a person forever. Some try to hide their culture, embrace it, or even ignore where they came from in the first place. I could say so many ugly things about culture but many beautiful ones as well. It seems with today's modern society that whenever culture clashes, there is an instinctual action that is decided and is so righteously named violence. Every day is a new shooting, a body bag to film, and there is a constant gap between the communication of different cultures that seems to never vanish with time. There is no peace without blood; there is no racism without misunderstanding and no culture without difference.

I do not want to generalize or blame anyone for the attacks on people of different cultures, but I demand to know why we all cannot act like civilized beings. It's rather simple to get along with people of different cultures and yet there is this bitter rage at seeing a person's apparent difference that it motivates people to do horrible, unspeakable things. Every time I hear about a tragedy or another racist argument that has ended in death, I just become sicker at the thought of what it is like to live with the lack of humanity in this world.

When children have the upbringing to yell "Hey white woman" to a passing stranger who is just trying to go about their day is when I then become concerned for the state of this world. Yes, it is true that a person is white and is a woman, but the better question might be what is her name? A name shows a cultural background and allows for individuals to connect beyond their visual perceptions of each other. Instead of looking in negativity about the things that make up a person's identity, try to understand why they do those things. I mean honestly, are you seriously going to go up to a person and ask, why are you black? That is just stirring up trouble and asking to be slapped right there.

I mean we do not just go up to a person and ask people why they are a certain color, but we should start a conversation like what is your cultural background? Seeing the beauty in what makes a person different opens doors for so many possibilities you never realized. Being able to taste and sense the richest, deepest parts of a person's culture and to experience it is an improvement from a person firing a gun in violent misunderstood anger to the realization that there is value in every culture. Yes, it is not easy to forgive past cultural misgivings between our ancestors and whatever violence that has occurred in the span of a thousand years, but it just gets old after a while to hate what makes other people different. There is so much more growth that comes from embracing people of different cultural backgrounds that you might find yourself along the way as well.

So, what is culture? It is not just the backgrounds we come from but an entire lifetime of everchanging events resulting in different beliefs, opinions, and habits. When you see something that you admire about another person, you tend to adopt that as a part of your persona in order to improve one's character in life, as life is a learning experience. Especially, when interacting with friends, you recognize that there is something unique about their difference that you cannot even call it difference anymore. In fact, it just becomes a reality and who that person is to you because you love them enough to see beyond what makes them different and accept them for who they are which is more than a person.

The inherent quality of a human being is not determined by just what is seen by others but by the steps they take when no one is looking to become themselves. The thing that one should choose to recognize in others is to see the best in them so that others who fail to see what you see in them at first will soon see it too. The greatest cultural accomplishment is helping others to transform themselves and showing them the positive traits you have experienced from them and to encourage them to share what makes them different from the world. Difference is not a flaw but a beautiful experience that we see in others and wish that they would share with us as well. That is what culture really is, sharing a part of yourself with others so that they may understand what it is like to stand in your shoes as a part of that culture.

In all, culture is the growth that starts with the simple conversation of asking someone their name. When you look, and face differences with arms open wide you will see what I see, the beauty of this world and that understanding will end every battle people start as cultures clash. We embrace others, we find ourselves, and that is how every culture should strive to be! Culture is an earnest love for one's origins and the origins of others, and to respect the hard work that came into making that beautiful, wonderful person. So, embrace, become and seek new cultural experiences as often as you can, and share who you are with the world to become yourself, cultured.

Chapter 5

Violent Meaningless Words

There is nothing more worthless than using bitter words to achieve a violent objective or to express the impudent lens with which one views the world. As a person who has emotions and is imperfect, I can tell you there is nothing more despicable than to use words in such a way to achieve violent ends. Based on observation, people tend to use words so casually that they make all efforts to say things violently and fail to observe the disastrous consequences of such actions. While it is not easy to be peaceful and humble all the time, it is more profound to use words to work for peace instead of violence.

If you look at an argument that has occurred you will find that there are many ways to end the story. Violence, compromise, or peace are three of the main options to stop an argument but however, peace is the best way to solve the problem. If you compromise yourself and settle for only half of a goal, you give up the values you have been fighting for to achieve a temporary end. Not all compromises are permanent, and a single violent word can fan the flames of compromise to transform into a bitter, bloody storm, incapable of only being ended with time. Because time signifies death, the death of ideas that caused people to disagree on something and there is just a strained gap left from the footsteps of those who just wanted to make a difference in their everyday lives. (I.e. The human condition)

Compromise only leads to more arguments that eventually vanish with a breath of wind, showing that peace is the best solution to every problem. Although it is not the only option, the best way to compose a message and to speak it to others is to do so peacefully. Peace is not an out of control protest that transcends into uncontrollable fire and looting that is disgraceful to every enlightened human who watches in embarrassment as the peace they just worked for becomes jaded and ruined. No pacifist individual wants to see peace become a shield for allowed violence that seeks to undermine the right of people to live quietly. I have watched my city burn, with the forefronts of anger echoed in the undefined banner of misguided peace and it disgusts me to see what peace has become today. Not a symbol of eternal light and hope, but peace has been torn in the shrewd pages of a book that kills anyone who disagrees with it. Indeed, peace has become devoured by the violent nature of the masses who wished away their freedom to only become violent hollow shells of what a real person is.

The real person uses words like stop your anger, understand the hearts of others, and even if you hate me, I will still love you no matter. The great blue heron that soars over the wet marshland spreads peace and with every wing stroke of air ends the violence carved in the hearts of those who shed their feathers of freedom a long time ago. Freedom is not a measure for violence but a way out, to tell the truth and to do so in a manner that exhibits only the behavior of the great blue heron. We are not meant to be violent people but with every word we take for granted and spit into the eyes of our enemy, then really, we no longer deserve the right to be called peaceful.

For when you look upon the depths of human suffering, there is a constant wish for an end to it all. Yet the answer for suffering is not an end but a realization that to prevent the suffering of others we must work to achieve peace. Violence not only drives more violence, but it isolates the common goal that we are searching for which is peace. I have found that in trading suffering for peace and peace for suffering, that we sacrifice our animosity for each other in other to bring a great change to this world.

Suffering is a part of peace because it means giving up the violent outbursts of one's inner emotion to create a new outcome. The new outcome that results from choosing to give up violence is a happier world. The reality today is that with every second people are using violent, hateful, and acrimonious words to depict how they feel about each other, which is so wrong. As civilized beings, we need to have control over our tempers; otherwise, how can we teach the next generation to do so as well. The world that I experience from my window is paved with vicious insults, racist letters, and the reckless ramblings of the uneducated and poorly minded individuals who have chosen to ignore what really matters.

The thing that is key to ending any war is a willingness to understand the situation and to be able to give an accurate analysis without bias. Because the most important thing now should be God. The champion at ending violence is the Lord, Our God who strove to make people understand themselves and the lives of those that surrounded him. There is no better example of a peacemaker than Jesus who hung out with sinners to reach them with his enduring message of peace and love. We will find that there is a peaceful message as well that we must give to this world. I am not saying that all things must be solved peacefully, but I am stating that the best way to end conflict is through harmony.

If you think that cursing and yelling at each other has merit, well I will say this, and that is such thinking is entirely useless. It is useless to argue when using violent words because nobody is going to respond positively to that, well unless you are Christian of course. However, the goal of conversation should be an agreement that the end of any argument must be met with peace. Do you know that old saying, "Speak or forever hold your peace" is very righteous you know? Before opening those wide jaws of yours to say something, consider how your words contribute to a conversation and whether you can say something to keep the peace.

Peace is not some sort of joke created to serve humanity at every whim and tossed out until it has value again. No! Peace is the reason why people have been able to coexist for so many years and anyone who threatens peace is met with suffering. Every person is drawn to some aspect of peace, and that's why peace is universal. As such, peaceful words end violence and the best way to live life is to do so in tranquility.

Part 2: The Price of Peace

But with every period of peace comes a price that many are not willing to say. Sometimes the price of peace is the lives of others given in a single moment to protect the way in which others want to live in this world. Like I said, in this society, there can be no peace without sacrifice, and sometimes the greatest way to achieve lasting peace is through death. Be it the death of one or the deaths of many, a person's quality of life depends on the giving of others. I live in a nation full of stories where people have given their lives to save their friends so that they can continue living in peace.

The saddest thing I have seen is when those who sacrifice everything for the sake of another's peaceful life are forgotten within the many distractions of this world. Visit a graveyard and reflect upon the lifetimes of lives who shed their existence so that the coexistence of others will never end. If you think that the common man is but a soldier of burden, stare upon the lives of those who never made it back to the shore to live your peace. That is why when we act in violence, we are shitting upon the memories of those who had to act violently for there to be any sign of peace. The truest sign of peace is the bones buried into the ground, etched memories of names long forgotten, who died in the line of duty trying to restore harmony to our world.

So, destroy those violent words that I know are hiding in your heart, and seek to understand the sacrifice made in violence, to become peace. For the only thing that God ever asked of you was "to be at peace". Live, learn, love, and remember that to live is to understand and respect the sacrifice of peace. So, trade-in your suffering for understanding and violence in for peace, and this is the beginning of meaningful words.

Chapter 6

The Beginning Of My Thoughts About Hope

So, in this world, exists the infeasible emotion of Hope. Thousands have felt it, millions have examined it, and yet none are close to what my take on Hope is. If you look at this world full of selfishness and giving people you can often wonder where to draw the line about who has hope and who does not. The truth is we all have hope, in its past form "hoped", in the present tense "hope" and regarding the future "hopes". So, we have hope, have hoped, and hold hopes from the past, present and future.

When we look to the past, we are faced with a constant truth about who we were then. As people, we were trying to become better than what we were, trying to just get through another day or were looking brightly on ahead and yet life is not what we had hoped then either. It's better! Because we have lived to have hope in the present surging through our veins to push us onto the next scene. With hope comes an uncertain direction that we are taking on to wish our way to the top. However, there are those who just hope to continue to live their life in the present, as it is peaceful and quite lovely. Yet there are the even stranger others who seem to want to do everything in the world to become who they truly are. There is that promise of a new direction that pushes them to not just have hope but to continue to have hopes for the future whether they be different or not.

It seems that knowing the gentle reminder that the future is uncertain, is what pushes people to have even greater hopes for their futures. Because hopes in turn change form into dreams that are within the grasp of anyone if they work hard enough to dare to achieve them. So, you see my thought-on hope is that it is a beautiful thing to have for we can choose to store it for later as well. That is right hope is like wonderful energy that surges from our bodies to invigorate and strengthen our will to survive. Sometimes, hope is just happiness in a daze like a dream, imagining all the things you are about to achieve. In fact, I miss hope, that feeling of glorious soaring into my body at the burst of a moment of emotion, to force me to realize that this world is not just about me.

This world is about the pursuit of something more that we are all desperately searching for. Some hope for things to get better and for the world to turn the hands of fate in their direction for a change. The greatest part about hope is that it is not a definitive promise and can evolve at any time to adapt to how a person is feeling at any stage of time. Ah, how I love the person who created hope, the great God himself. In fact, the only true hope worthy of having is faith in his Son, the Lord, Our God. You know the one all the Christians call the Savior and Lord that you casually toss out at any time until he is useful again for you. Well, I truly love the Lord whose life is far greater than mine and is my source of hope for everything. Those strong bear-like arms that he possesses to reach out for you in an embrace of love, that allows people to just forget for a second that life is unfair at all.

Chapter 7

Words and this World

I n this world, there are those born to be different from all others. These people are the ones who look through the glass window down at the rest of society and wish they could be a part of that world. Belonging to a group of individuals that smile, care for each other, and stare into the abyss seems to be some sort of forceful wish that will never be achieved for them because they do not belong to this world. They are the words, the people who take on strands of shielded syllables to become meaning to those who would not otherwise understand them.

The ones whose figures soar on the invisible currents of air fronts to reach the curved structure of another's ear that is what these words are. The words are the ones who look and just feel something more from this world because they do not belong to it and yet society does not accept them as such. The world is not kind to those who are different, and there is this rush to get rid of the divergent streak within everyone. If one is not able to speak and whistle to the tunes of the world's songs and join them as such, they become erased measures of leady black on a page falling to the ground to just be hurt again. You see words and the world have no place with each other because the world will only taint the words further, causing them to become less than what it is they are.

Society cannot accept what words are, so they make it their prerogative to silence any anomaly that threatens the perfectly running engine of the tightly oiled machine that is society. Because there is no place for words that attack like pierced starry thorns to take down the lies of this world, society says there is no room for me. For I am the words, they silence at every moment and the tongue they cut out with bloody scissors to bleed away the wrongs that I have clearly committed for being born different. Yet I am the one who looks out the glass window, and nobody can hear my lighted cries for help because they do not care. I do not know what divides me, the words, and this world, but clearly there is something wrong with both of us. Are we star crossed lovers that fate has forcibly divided into destinies that are designed to drive each other away forever? I do not remember what part of me divided me from this world, but I can tell you the day I became separated from them all. Elementary, fourth grade, I was the most used word in the class surrounded by the seeds of punctuation. Yet how did it become this? The greatest, longest word, torn into shrivels by a messed-up sleepover that ended in the mother of punctuation screaming at me, " Monster", "don't associate with that one". I remember it all the jagged threads of glasslike shards surging from my eyes as I was tossed aside and forced into the path of the clearly defined intellectual.

This is what the world does to words! It takes them and favors them for a time and then blows them away on the lip strings of the wind until they are needed again. Yet the strangest thing is when these words create works of great beauty and interest to society; then they again become valued in the hearts of others. What kind of a system is this that constantly takes and pulls apart the pieces of a puzzled person who just wants to coexist but cannot because it is not time for society to take them back yet and value them again. It is like a loveless man begging to be taken back into the arms of his loyal woman and yet keeps going back and forth until that woman finally breaks apart and becomes loveless too. I am not saying this is the case in every situation, but I am saying there is no reason for treating words this way.

Words cannot just be used repeatedly if the owner is not going to take sincerity in accepting these words for what they are. The world has a personal system of vendettas against people like me who are the words, and once they think you will not fit in with them, then you are gone. Is it perhaps the fault of the words that they cannot understand friendship? Is friendship not an exchange of love and equality and acceptance? Well I did all this and still was thrown out by my best friend and the world. The world does not favor the words of those who have not established themselves, and rarely does it accept the different for what they are, that is different.

The word different and the world is just a tragedy waiting to happen, for both cannot coexist without being absorbed into each other and becoming something new. What that something is though, I do not know but supposedly it's better than being at odds with the world every day. You don't know how exhausting it is to dodge through crowds of angry voices and pointless stares just wanting to say something about what you are, but there is nothing, just silence, no words for the individual that doesn't fit in with this society. As such, there is just a word looking at the world and the world blinking back as if to say, " I know what you are and that's not me", so goodbye.

Part 2: How I claim to know the world

So, you may ask how I claim to know the world? How could I not know this world in which I live, breathe, and experience every day. That which I look upon from the lens of the inavoidant stranger who can only look, listen, and see that which the world wants them to see. There are many things that this stranger's lens may want to be involved in, but they are excluded from such things according to society's rules. Society's rules that detest the human being who is alone and left out of a group and cannot even get into one without hearing the inner voices of people, looking, shouting in anger at them for not ascribing to their intelligence or to fit in with the herd/ hive-like mindset of them all. The way that a person is measured is not by their capabilities but by their ability to belong. And even if that person is a capable leader and intelligent person, there will always be this inner barrier of stored hatred for their gifts. To live for me is to not understand why I feel this hatred towards working in groups with others and they always feel this shredded hatred towards me as well for not being the person they want. I do not get it! Why is it so hard for me to work with other people, yet everyone else can just speak to each other and say the words they want to? It is like when people get to me, they just stop trying to interact with me as a person.

Do they not understand that people are different too? That it chokes me up in my throat at the pain of not being able to belong in a society with people who have friends and can belong to a world that is not so different from mine. What people have forgotten is that different human beings want the same kind of love and respect that they should enjoy as a part of society. I can't quite gauge why there is this disconnect between me and others, but I do know that this world is a hard

K.M.F

place to live in and yet we must stay strong in order to meet the people who will eventually accept and love us for who we are.

However, there is always going to be a difference between words and the world. Words have an impact upon the world, and the words must decide if they will let the world impact them as well. It is not enough to have claimed to have seen the world, but I can tell you I have seen my world. My world is one filled with dark trees, and mechanical Machines and loud noises whose voices trample over the insignificant being that is supposed to be me. I try my hardest not to stand out upon humanity, yet my personality and intelligence makes me a target for most of this world. I do not get why the world seeks to despise that which is different from them, but I guess that is just the way the world is and has always been. However, it is easy to denounce the world with doses of negativity and to forget the general kindness that is shattered upon the least of us by the more fortunate others. I think that the fundamental message of this world is to be kind to others without hurting them, but I do not see this kindness in my world; I often end up messing up this kindness somehow.

Everywhere, every hall of a city possesses this stare that bores into the brows of my back; I can just feel the fiery indifference directed at me from any distance. I am not going to excuse myself, however and say I have no part in the bitter

42

hatred that is directed at me because when all eyes are on me, in truth, I hate them too. I grin, and I snarl my sovereign face at those who oppress me and yet within my heart is this desire to love them despite their unyielding attempts to throw the gaze of death upon me in punishment. I question whether, I can really coexist in a society that I don't understand, that which gazes at me in their unnatural angst and pain when really all I want is to understand what it's like to be a good friend. Yet to me it takes a lifetime to understand what friendship really is. So, what is friendship?

Chapter 8

How To Spot Friendship In Words

Theme is no easy approach to friendship especially when it comes to understanding it. There is a constant struggle between man and Earth going on in a friendship where one person is bound to another and to their duties to both heaven and this Earth. The question is, is friendship something worth putting into words so beautiful that the Earth may understand it? Is it something that can be auctioned off to the highest bidder where only one benefits from this supposed symbiotic relationship when it is one-sided? Friendship depends on who you are, who you are with, and who you want to become. It is not as easy as saying we are friends because true friendship takes much more than words. You can say "we're friends," but you can't say " I will be there" when really you are a million miles away in some separate dimension that will never, ever include me.

Friendship is not just an equation for success; it is not just simply acquiring another item and painting it into a picture of implied perfection. Because the truth is when you try to paint friendship as this picture of boundless graceful that will always be entangled in your heart, your lying about it. Friendship is a lie. It's not even what its word really means; its pain, its beauty, its hell, pouring out all your love into another person, hoping, praying, they might accept you for who you are. The difference between true friendship and the stuff that we all lie about and claim is perfect is this; time. Time is the difference between reason and companionship; it divides the category of friendship into a loyal friend and compassionate stranger. Because even if you pour out all your heart in a year onto a person, they will still abandon you. There is no off-switch to this disconnect; it simply happens when someone has decided you are not one of their kind, that is it, the end of our friendship.

This is what friendship is; a constant game of tug and war between 2 hearts until one of you finally has had enough. I know this seems like such a negative, biased view of friendship, and I might be the rare exception but let me tell you being a good friend is not easy. Most of the time it could be happy, meow a buck, and yet other times it is a plague that ruins your life until you cannot even decide who you want to be anymore. To open your heart to another has its own risks and benefits; somehow it seems that friendship is not that worth it to me. Not with its pain and hurts, to the point where it feels like the

45

pressure is beating on my lungs, collapsing my knees, until I am just on my own again, gasping for air at the ends of a bridge that had fallen already so long ago. So, the question is, is there a positive side to friendship? Somewhere in our hearts is there room in our emotionally damaged room for our friends? Well, there is room in our hearts if we are willing to forgive and move on again and love the other parts of people as well. As people we spend our lives trying to find that thing we have in common so strongly with others that we miss out on the one part that unites us all and that is our connection to belief in Our God.

Do not tell me you do not believe in anything, how else did all of us get here? I do not care about what thoughts you have on how we were created, for the truth is we all come from God. He created us, shaped our minds and hearts to become the beautiful people we are today. We may live in a lake of uncertain floods and fields of darkening stars, but still, there is a line between the two that draw us back to God. So, tell me which is your line? What is your belief, my brothers and sisters? Those same stars and pieces of wood that you bow before are merely tools created by a God so long ago that we even forgot his name. But on the road of life, his face shines in the soil, calling our hearts back to him, calming our steps and waiting on us to become the friend he wants to be. Because there is nothing like it in this world that is a truer example of friendship than the loving smile of the Lord, our God. So praise him, don't shame him, lift up your worries to him, and he will be there in a flash to be your sword, shield, your hidden arms saying that we will fight the battle of this world together, Amen. It is what is in my heart; through these words I hope you will understand the power of God, your friend and protector forever if you want him to be that. Because God is our friend, we must love him as a true friend does, and the greatest thing is that he will never forsake or abandon us and our lives as our lives are of value to him because we are friends.

What's great about a relationship with God is he has promised to never forsake us or abandon us and this is sealed through our bond of friendship, the covenant of the rainbow, the sign in the sky that ties us to God for sure. Think of the most beautiful thought you have heard of or had about life and ask yourself where such beauty comes from. Is it from the rocks, the trees, the stars? No, this feeling of utter peace and sobriety comes from the one true God who loves you unconditionally. For the love of God is forever and it will never be destroyed. God is love, the friend who will not sleep until you are safe inside of your home until you finally come home to him.

There is not much more to it, to be honest, because it is up to you to decide whether you want a personal relationship with God or not. To be without God and have him as a friend is a dangerous thing because you feel all alone and that there is no one out there to advocate for you and to fight for you as well. A part of friendship is the battle against the world together, with your deep connection and marvel at what grace it is to be able to exist and write your story in this world. Because friendship is in its self-words, patterned on a page, bringing to others the greatest tales of an adventure that has long been forgotten but is remembered by these blocks of words, A memory of momentous laughter between people should be recorded and written down in the analects of history so that it will be there later in time for another person to view and see and maybe laugh too. This is the value of the historian who records every figment from the minds of those he observes to see what truly the best parts of people are and what are not. Because the best parts of people are the ones you should remember the most in friendship, and in which you will tell the stories of these times to the next generation too. And right now, I look at this world full of running cars and rockless faces that do not look friendly, who seem to have forgotten what real friendship is. It seems that when we try to give rise to the lies of relationships that make up our life, we give up on what the real truth is; the trust between friends fails to even measure what the lie of friendship is.

So, what is real friendship? Is it more than just two people joined for the benefit of another day? Well I say friendship needs a new name! Friendship needs to be called more than just a thing or two, but it should be called truth. Friendship needs to be called the true relationship, the truth that when you share a part of yourself with another, they should return it equally in kind. There can be no one side that is greater than the other because that is just another concept called dependency. I am not saying that you should not rely on your other part, but that each person needs to be responsible for the other. Love each other equally and do not let the blackness of this world tear apart your connection, and no matter what, do not forget to be honest with each other. Relationships involve truth, and you must value that which seems important in your partner, for that person has offered up a piece of themselves to you. Treat that new piece of you as an extension of your own body and remember it for without this understanding there can be no friendship; no minds are one, they are two. The essential message is that you should treat people with deep love, and they will want to be your friend. Make exceptions for others, and you will find yourself filled with a spirit of love and a pocket full of the numbers of the truthful, Amen. Thus, it is the end of the lies of friendship and the start of a truthful relationship that is fully embodied in love, the new true ship. The ship that will sail away with two and come back with more is the one you want to get on. So be a good friend!

Chapter 9

Love, Life, And Choice

Ah, the one chapter of this supposed story called life that I was looking forward to writing which is the difference between love and choice. When it comes to love, it seems we all have this choice about whom to love, how to love, and what counts as love and what is just a farce. Let us start with what love is. According to the tales of our life, love seems to be this thing personified as magic only for us to realize in our later years how false this story really is. Love is not simply; boy meets girl, they fall in love and spend eternity together. You see the truth about love is that love ends, and you might not think about it, but it ends fast. Regarding human understanding there seems to be a limit to love but what about the divine? Is there a limit to the divine love of God? Do you think the most powerful being in the world who coined the term love did not create it? Well, the answer lies in the bastions of the question of love for what true love is there other than God. God is love because he created it, bled for it, with the tears of anguish felt in his vast heart of cloudless skies and empty heavens waiting for a son he wanted to return. For the glory of a father is his one and only son, who came down to the Earth, bore our sin and fate so that we might come back to him again. He, the one I refer to is the great God, our Father whose cries are felt all the way from heaven as he sees the ones he created out of love suffer for him and for others. So the part of love, I want you to understand is not to suffer for love but to suffer because of a deeper connection in your heart that leads you to praise that he is the one true God! Let those words leave your lips, and I can guarantee he will change your life through those words for the spirit of God will enter and live in you forever if you do. It's like this great gift wrapped in silver blood-reddening bows that tell you what sacrifice, what the essence of love really is. Because love is sacrifice, it's suffering to the point that nobody can bring you back from the groundless remains of your faith that remain. For faith is a matter of death, yet, you defy death because you are saved through faith in the Lord, Jesus Christ who died on the cross so that you may live. I understand this may like a complicated process or a bit insane but let me tell you it is not. I cannot imagine a day in my life anymore without God being bearing down my back and watching over me like the sun shading the trees from the vagrant storm. There is no need for such analogy, but the Lord, my God, is the one who took me out into the light like a small child lifted into the sun to touch the sunrise that remains. For like I said, someday that light will end, and this world will be filled with darkness unlike you have ever seen or known before. There will be no safety, no security, everywhere the flags of Christians will burn, and whatever will remain is hate reigning supreme. But soon that dark will be snuffed out and destroyed burned and broken into pieces that will never again obey the commands of the one who created them, for they will cease to exist. Will you be one of those pieces? Make up your mind because I am seriously concerned for you and the fate of others in this world. I have seen the kindness in each one of your souls, and I want to save that one part that might be good of you. For soon, I am leaving my friends to a land far away, that I have no idea about either, I can only promise that it's good, better than this world now. There will be no promise of pain, no promise of forgiveness, for those who do not obey the commands of God because God watches every day. I want you to come with me to this beautiful faultless world filled with the faces of angels dressed in white robes freely waving strands of pine and sagebrush to the wind, for this is the true vision I have seen so far and heard about of heaven, it's in the Bible. Yet my responsibility is heavy because I am to drag you to this place, I must. I can't see my children on the street running around like sheep unable to come back to me, with the sign of the moon in their eyes, they don't seem to know who I am and it breaks my heart to see how broken they are inside. I want them to come and find rest in me, but they walk away into the pitch-black sunspots and ignore the mirror of what I am saying. For I too, am a mother who watches this world and tries to nurture it from the hands' God gifted me with, yet there is this greater force that seems to stop me from reaching you with these words. Your too busy with the next fancy of your mind, or whatever it is this world seems to offer in pleasure, to listen to one who sincerely wants to help you see the promise of heaven through faith in God's son Jesus. I just want to bang on the glass some more and get you to look at me, to look at what I'm saying, but you always just walk away from me, and I know this is not love. Love is not a silence that gradually just starts to fade away back into the quiet recesses of mind because you can no longer speak about who you are anymore. You do not know who you are anymore, beneath the featherlike weight of a boulder on your back that just says go away, I do not want to be saved. I do not need to be saved because inside I just want to die anyway. But I want to take you with me. Oh! What am I to tell him when I lay at the feet of God, and you are not there? Yes, you my friend, the six million strangers who read this book, whoever you are, how am I supposed to explain to God why I did not try to save you. When he asks where is Joel? What am I supposed to tell him? Where are they, Katie? Where were you when they needed you? The only thing I can do is to sit in the silence of my shame and sorrow and tell him that I failed they are dead; I am sorry, God. They will not come no matter how much I beg and plead and kneel at their knees; they are not coming back! I wish that I could take every one of you with me to this miraculous place where there is no pain, no hunger, and only a boundless spirit of love and energy that fills your heart; oh God what am I going to tell him. How am I going to tell him beautiful June with the pretty curls and bright laugh is not coming home to heaven. I can only let tears slide down my face for even I do not know how to forgive such a thing. This is the pain every Christian bear in their hearts; we only want the best for you, even if it breaks our hearts and bodies to see you come to heaven. To part with your soul is so unbearable, can you imagine going to a place like heaven and your mother, father, or anyone else you love not being there? Is not love wanting to be with those you care about forever? Well, real love is staking your life on the permanent promise that can only be brought from belief in Jesus, the one who bore pain on the cross for you so that you may believe in him and be saved through the love that was his sacrifice in blood. Real love comes through pain and something that Jesus once said was, "There is no greater love than to lay down ones lives for one's friends," Do you want to know love? Know Jesus! The living testament of what it means to be love, to embody love, God is love, and

Jesus is our God, the Lord. God lives in him, and he lives in us. Thus we have received the right to call ourselves children of God by placing our faith in him. So now, what do we do with this love? Well, we share it with others, the message of God's love because we want to take others with us to heaven as well. I cannot imagine heaven without my loved ones and to experience the beauty of utopia without them seems a choice too selfish too bear. It is one thing to bear the responsibility of telling others about God so that they will believe in him, and it is another to deny them the knowledge of it. So, therefore, I tell you that the Lord says whoever believes in him will see Heaven today. For life cannot be measured in the single second of a day and love cannot be spoken with the few actions of a letter, so too is it God's love that you must know before it's all over. There is no end to God's love, but there is an end to you. So, choose love or to die, buried in the memories of some sad fool that failed to remember you, I will not remember you. But I will never forget those that died not knowing the love of God or ignored the promise of something better because they only wanted to lean on their own understanding. I may whisper onto your lips the secret to eternal life or shout it in the streets, but I cannot choose it for you; that's why love is a choice, and there is no greater impact I can have on you than to tell you to choose to believe in the love and peace that comes from the Lord. So, love is peace, and God is choice, so I believe you will choose heaven in the end, Amen. I will be waiting for you at the gates, meet me their proud soldiers of light, my Christian brothers, and sisters, so sayeth, Sister, Hope, once again Amen.

Chapter 10

Words as Relaxation

S omehow, I cannot find words to describe this feeling today. I have tried changing the music yet there is nothing I feel, nothing I have no words for this tired feeling where words are nothing to me anymore. Even listening to guys singing in Korean while being half-naked, does nothing to echo this feeling of wordlessness inside my heart. So, what do you do when you have no words, no love, or energy to pour into your work anymore? The truth is that you write, you take those fingers of yours and grab a pen and just sit down and write the day away. Because as people we must accept that there is a part of ourselves that needs to be relaxed, and yet at the same time exercised in order to make any progress in the day; want to know what the most relaxing word is in the world? It's lazy.

That feeling when you just want to take a load off, pack up the bricks and things and just lay down and watch the sun at a beach. The way I feel right now is not so different from how you feel because it is a natural thing to want to be lazy; in fact, its hidden potential lives inside of all of us. You see the funny thing is I cannot make lazy an academic concept, because well it's just who we are; it is okay to be lazy sometimes and watch the television because it's something you deserve. Do not let people say the word work to you on a lazy day because it just kills the mood. As a resident mood-killer myself, I can safely say it's better to accept that part of yourself instead of just trying to change it. There are plenty of people who will tell you get up, get motivated and yet they are the most unmotivated individuals you know.

Do not let the opinions of others determine the course of how you're going to live your life for words are the thing we can never take back. We cannot in our moments of indignation rule out who we want to be because of a few stray words. What I am saying is there is a time to shut out everything and embrace the silent relaxing part of the world because words do not talk all the time. In fact, words do not talk at all, their inanimate and so are their creators. In this moment of panic, we need to realize that sometimes the key to success lies not in how much effort we put into something but the quality of the work there. This advice that is coming from an overachiever might cause you to tumble back into your seat, but I often wonder what would happen if we threw away our words for a second and just relaxed in the moment of truth. What is the potential for such an idea? I have asked, is there a positive benefit from relaxing while still working hard? I am always stressed by the expectation, swallowed by my accomplishments, and then spit out to repeat the process all over again. I wish I had the luxury to stop in my tracks for a moment and really consider what I am doing so much work for. Besides my future, who else will look upon these accomplishments with pride and say I am glad to have known that person. Will they be relieved at knowing I lived such a prosperous life or be freaked out by all the effort, it took to get there, out of my own family, I am the only academic born over the centuries. The others wasted their gifts and were simply unmotivated to try harder to reach their full capabilities. Thus, their entire dreams and wants to have been placed on my shoulders because I am the only one capable of doing such work, and at the same time, I wish I had someone to share the burden with. The rest of my family is just normal, normal jobs, same-space retirement, etc. Why is all the stress placed on one person who just wants to get by and through the day? Do you feel an expectation? Well, do you? Do you feel what I feel when the whole world's weight is on your shoulders, and you just want people to understand that you are a person too? You do not know what it is like to be reminded every day of what you should be doing, even if that is what you are already doing. Nobody should have to live to face expectation because it isolates and kills the real person behind the glass mirror who is just wanting to breakthrough.

If we just relaxed and could pace carefully through the stress, then we as people might be able to live that expectation. You do not need to shove the broom down our throats when we are already clawing, breathing for air in our minds in a world that expects even more. Let children be children for God's sake; why do you get to choose their dream for them in the first place. They will just end up hating you themselves, whoever they can get the anger out on. I have been learning a lot about anger lately, and I would argue that the one thing that frustrates people the most is an expectation. My God why do you people constantly feel the need to reiterate the things you want us to do when we will do it on our own time! We are individuals not slaves to the will of others, and how we choose to live our lives is ultimately up to God. You see God owns a part of us that no one can take away which is why as people we need to value God's plan for our future. Do not deny there is a God that exists because if so, you're denying your existence. As people, we need to acknowledge how we came into this world, so we know how we're going to want to leave it as well. I am not saying the voices around you don't matter, but I am saying, Listen to God, Relax and let him whisper in your ear worlds that you could have never imagined on your own. Be at peace with yourself (your person), and you will find a whole world filled with doors and windows that open to the great above. I know it's no easy task to believe in God, but it's the best thing you can do for your life so that you can become who we all are and that is children of God. The thing is that God sees every aspect and inches into your life so unexpectedly; it is a miracle. Let me tell you, God came into my life when I could no longer love myself and yet at the same time chose to love me is what God did. It was dark and storming one night, after being betrayed by one I loved, and yet God came to me because I asked him to. If you ask, you shall receive guidance, and that's how progress is made, but there is the question of application. How do we relax and not let others expectation get to us while also believing in something that seems so impossible? The answer is trust, that you must trust that there is a God and that he has a plan for you beyond the expectation of things others dream, For there is a difference between expectation and God's plan for your life. While you may expect or others expect success, God is willing to love you for both your success and failure. Today, it seems that there is a weight placed on people to earn the most money, which seems to be the only thing that matters. I know you say that money cannot buy happiness, well it seems this thought is false. Money is a thing that thy quote "makes the world go round," and we have built our society around the expectation that we all want to earn money. Because money is life, often money is the expectation;

what a shallow way to live yet we know we need this expectation to live. This word, this money and if we do not have it, we are no better than the beggars in the street, living off the wages of others. And so, we work, if not for what to live another day, to meet the expectation that society lumped on us to earn that last slice of money, the wage that guarantees survival as well. I get it though; I am so pissed off when I see the hobo in the street wasting that scrap of money that you just gave to them all because they're too lazy to earn their own.

Well speaking as one whose mother threw her to the street, I can tell you what it feels like to be homeless. Because the truth is were all homeless wandering souls scampering too like the hobo after the last scrap of money, no I need faith to just survive. Yet where is the plan for freedom in this? Where is the plan for joy, creativity, love, art if our lives are only systems of productivity? No one just wants to work themselves to death to the point they do not even feel at home anymore. Although you may have a nice fancy house with a piano in it, right across the street is a person living in that obscene box you glare at every day as you pass by. Heck, we're all envious, jealous creatures who stare out the windows of our minds, chasing the next golden opportunity that comes our way. I have gone from poor to providence in the span of four short years of suffering, and yet I am still unhappy; I am still unsatisfied with what I have. I want to be in China, I want to be in any place, but here and yet this place is where I call home. I was called here by God, told here to stay, brought to my knees, screaming for breath by the expectation of this work.

Don't disobey God folks, follow him and let him help make your paths straight, because if you don't you might end up like Jonah in the body of a whale, somewhere gasping for air within the thick succubus like the trail of your sin, crushed under the whaling intestine of God's mighty fist upon your soul. So be at peace, and obey God, live for his plan, not for people's expectation, and relax knowing that you are always at home with God. For God is the house of love, and he will call you like me back to his house someday. Amen.

Chapter 11

Fighting A Bleeding Battle

E ver seen that longing in the brownish eyes of a woman, who is constantly looking into the distance? Well I see that in the eyes of Virginia Woolf who looks at me with eyes questioning what kind of a battle I am leading. The truth is I am fighting a bleeding battle that is personified through the eyes of the hourglass, which drips its pagan blood into the cylinder, hoping, praying, for the wound to close and heal right then and there. You may be asking what this crazy book is about, why is this author constantly going on and on about words. Well, the reality is that my words have the power to strike a blow into the sides of the enemy, and now you ask who the enemy is? Is it the oppressor, the loneliness I am battling? Or is it none of these? Is what you are fighting just the over bitter blackened taste of the thing that takes you over and makes you say unimaginable things, words like I hate you, I will kill you, makes you think thoughts of violence against a neighbor who has wronged you.

The truth is we are all born into this world, with two sides, the good and the bad, due to our ancestors fall long ago.

Our ancestors sinned, and now we are tainted with sin too, because it's our history, our fault too. Yup that voice in our heads screams it's our fault we're not good enough for God to love, and well we do not belong in this world; it is bad to not belong to this world. Let me tell you this, voice has a name, and it's Satan the devil, you know, the controller of Hell, who is always hungry for more companions to join him. Let me tell you; my biggest struggle is with the lies he told me, forced me to know, and remember all of the evil events in life because the truth is, I can never forget. I can never forget as a young girl, my mom beating the dog to death with a broom handle and wanting to throw myself at her to stop them. I cannot forget the tears of my soul when looking at the woman who beat my brothers, drugged us as kids, and even had the audacity to beat me with a shoe for cursing at her. I have so much anger, so many memories, of pain, hell I am fighting a bleeding battle with Satan. You see Satan wants me to forgive him for telling these lies, for introducing sin into the world and the truth is it isn't my job to call the shots on forgiveness, yet I can't blame him for everything. Life happens, this world is already turned upside down, and well I forgive him, I forgive them all. I forgive the memories so I can stop being tortured by them, and well I will let God deal with his creation. Because the truth is,

I do not have the will and the power to fight evil on my own. I need the Lord, Jesus Christ, my savior, the love and Lord of my life.

I can say with confidence it is only him who can forgive my sin, open my eyes, and make me see a beautiful world too. I have no other friend, than my brother at arms, the Lord, for he has saved my soul, such is the joy, the comfort, and energy that I get from him; praise the God above. I'm not saying this like I just believe in Jesus because he has provided for my life; I would believe regardless due to seeing him at work in this world and in me as well, through my life which is just amazing. I reminisce and draw you back to a time when I battled with the kind of anxiety that could have killed me. But the Lord came for me, sent his angel to help me out, and I can tell you I have seen the face of God without having seen it. God's heart is so big and vast that he loves all of us equally, and it's too much to take in. Oh, what the majesty and might of God is when I am fighting the bleeding battle because I know I will get through because I am fighting for God too. I am fighting to see the word of God alive in the hearts of this world, to inspire a revolution that changes us all. Because, no offense, but Satan is not where it's at. I don't care what he promised you, it's all lies; you know it's bad for you like McDonald's French fries; you take one bite and just want more until it becomes the poison that ruins your life forever. I beg you to take the antidote, do not give in and believe in the love of Christ Jesus because he died for you, to save you from your sins.

I cannot remember the last time a man loved me enough to offer his life up at the drop of a hat for our love. It just does not happen anymore, and yet Jesus is not just a man, he is the one and only son of God who fights the devil head on to save you from your sin. Do not listen to Satan because he only provides relief in the form of more sin and lies that will kill any chance you have of getting to experience the joys of heaven. Do not do it dear brother or sister, faith in Jesus is the last real saving grace. If I an imperfect, damaged person, can be saved so can you, too. I recently learned that it's not my fault if you don't go to heaven because I tried telling you constantly in this piece we are all fighting a losing battle with our words one we want to win so desperately. But please, friends, put down the pen, take a second and crack open a bible and get saved.

Please come with me my friends; I will face it with you, the bleeding battle of this world against Satan. Because the truth is this world is going to be destroyed soon, God has said it, and soon you will see it all blasted to pieces,our homes everything we own will be gone in the span of a thousand years, trust me Jesus is coming back someday to take us home to heaven. He will come in all his glory; you will hear the trumpet and look on in awe at his majesty, come to save us all. You shall bow down at his feet wearing white robes and waving palm branches because you know who the Lord is. Let us all believe and launch ourselves at his feet because truly it will be an amazing moment to see. And I will live to see it for sure because this, the battle to see God is worth fighting for. So why is it worth it? I bet you are wondering what I get out of this, and the simple answer is you get to live. You get to live forever worshipping God and enjoying the company of those you love forever.

The battle for God is a hard fight because the devil has a powerful influence over the minds of humans. But God is greater and stronger, and you will just need to learn to trust and believe in him. You may think that humanity can create amazing things alone, but this is nothing compared to what God can do if everyone had them in their lives. For right now is an age of unbelievable violence that humans enact against each other to gain some sort of advantage over others. Why all the violence, why all the the blood, my brothers, and sisters? Why are four people shot outside my house when one of those people could have been my brother coming home late from a Christian life group with his friends. Do I have to worry at night for the ones I love because yall just cannot live in peace? Is white powders, drugs, money all you guys care about? What happened to caring about people's lives? Because the truth is I love my brother and my father, all of my family, I don't want to burn their bodies and scatter their ashes to the wind because I need them; I need them because they're the only physical thing I can hold onto for as long as I want forever.

Do you not have something better to love than objects? Because my family and other people's families are not something for you to blow caps into, for me to wake up to their blood every day, as just another piece of damaged faith. And now, I must take up boxing, and learn how to shoot a gun, just to protect the only family I have in this world. Why don't you just come down and shoot me instead? You are shooting me in the heart when you try to take away the only things I love in this world; I don't want much at all, but just to come home to loved ones who hug me and tell me how much I mean to them. All of us want to be valued and loved, but we are too busy shooting other people's loved ones to care about what kind of a family we can have. The truth is if you need help, God is always there to provide you one. Because I do not just belong to an Earthly family, but I am a member of the family of God. I am a child of God because I believe in his Son, the Lord, and nothing; nobody can ever take him away from me, not even death.

I will protect God's chosen ones and lay down my life so that God's will may be done in their lives as well. The devil will not beat me today; he can bring any kind of suffering he wants; I will endure it all; Job did too and so can I. With every breath,

I will bleed to win against the forces of evil lead by Satan in this world. I do not fear you Satan; I do not fear death; nothing will ever separate me from God again. I do not care what riches you have to offer me; God's love is worth far more than any trinket filled with lies. I will not curse you, but I do warn you, my Lord, God is coming back someday soon, and you will never be able to hurt another loved one again. When I go to heaven, I will not remember you; I will be healed due to the blood of Jesus's sacrifice on the cross. I know I will be welcomed home into the house of God and vow to spend eternity serving him, doing no matter what it takes, I have sworn to take up my cross and bleed on it so the greater glory of God can be accomplished in this world. Do not think you have won because you will never win against the Jesus I know. The Jesus I know is pure, sweet, and innocent, and he didn't deserve to meet such a painful death on the cross, but he did it so that all of us and made the greatest sacrifice there ever was. Praise be to him who bled for us and won the battle that day. So, Amen. Blessed be the name of the Lord, our God.

Chapter 12

The End Of Words/ How To End Words

When looking at this, I do not know if there is a right way to end words. I always feel troubled when it comes to writing the conclusion of a paper. If you were to ask me, there are many endings to words that are punctuation like the subtle period or exclamation point. Often you can use a semicolon to expand your thoughts on an idea, but there is really no end or limit to our thoughts. All good stories have an end, a stop, not a cliffhanger; god I hate cliffhangers. It's like just write the damn book already why you got to torture us with an incomplete story. Lol writers, well when referring to the end of words, I am not specifically talking about how to end words with grammar, but about the end of a story. How do you want your story to end is my question? Do we get a choice in how we will die? The thing is all of these are great questions, but they do not really matter.

Our words do not end with us; they start to occur again in the mix of young people, as we have a chance to be an influence on this world. This is the reason I started writing this book because soon my story will die with me, but I do not want my words to. I do not want to be just some dime a dozen novel placed at the back of a shelf forced to collect dust until they burn me in the fire. Quite a terrible image is it not, burned in a fire because your time has run out, which sounds like creation. Lol. The power we have as people is to decide how we want to be remembered by the future generations in how we choose to live now. Will we live like fools and ignore the wisdom of God, and live on only what we have learned from this world? Or will we listen to the words of one greater than us, who died so that we could live eternally with him in heaven? It's your choice but like Joshua said, as for me and my family will worship the Lord. Because it's important to realize that the only one we need to live for is God. He will remember us the most because he created us, and he loves all of us equally.

The funny thing is after this world has been destroyed, the only thing we will have left is ourselves and God. So, if you want to be remembered as one who believed Satan's lies and disobeyed God, well into the fire you go. The sad thing is those who know Christ and yet love you must watch as you live a life of self-destruction and sin. It's hard to watch my mother everyday look at this world and not know Jesus's love and yet

I try to tell her all the time about him. The thing is she won't listen to me, and I do not know where she is going next. I can only hope it's heaven, and she realizes the words of God are true before it's too late and she is in the fire too.

Huh, funny is not fire the end of words too? Those engulfing flames of voices succeeding in muffling the letters of people who are not identifiable anymore. Book burnings, those vacant symbols of expression destroying the knowledge others worked so hard to achieve. I hate how the world burns the voice of what is different because it is not ideal at all. What is the ideal? How do we identify it? Is the ideal a carnage of letters, blotted out by the bluing hearts that dictate them so. I guess what I am trying to say is we decide the end of our words. Whether our words end in positivity or the negative it's our choice as no one has the right to take our words. And take them, they will and twist them into something so ugly and unidentifiable, and we just wonder why we even wrote them in the first place. I know everyone says once you say something, there is no way you can take it back, but the truth is we own our words. By owning our words, we are responsible for what we release into the world be it beautiful or not. Sometimes the reality is not beautiful; its not what people would expect from the casual observer of our world. As writers we are observers of words, of the truths in the world that the normal choose to ignore because it's inconvenient for them.

Really why is the truth inconvenient to them? I was told once that the greatest thing I could do was tell the truth, be it any truth especially about this world. This world I look out, and I see words everywhere; I hear them in the crowded classrooms of my university, in the hallways and I still wonder what really these people are thinking about this world. I do not know, but I do know what they are saying as they look at me with wandering eyes wondering where she is going. Well, the truth is I am staring back at you! I hear your words, and I realize that these could be the last words you speak too; these could be the last words I hear too.

So much value is placed on people's last words at the end of their lives that those words are said to be the most honest things they have spoken in their lives. How often are we truly honest about our lives until we face the end of them? As a person who has had many close encounters with death, it is a very scary thing. Seeing my grandfathers' lifeless body in a casket, I won't even tell you about the smell, but I do remember the candles. Such bright lights to celebrate the end of a life well-lived yet the only thing anyone could remember were his last words, the words they last said to him, and the moment he last saw them was the only thing I could think about as they lowered him into the ground forever. Often, I go back to his grave and speak to him and wonder if he is looking down at me from heaven above.

I do not know what his thoughts were on God, he left very few letters, but I remember his words. Therefore, we must value the end of our words and prepare them for the next generation who comes along. The goal is not to be selfish with our words and keep them to ourselves because we fear they will not make sense to the world or whatever lame excuse we come up with; that is the devil talking. He tries to drown out our words and convince us that no one will listen to our lives because they do not have any value. Value yourself, my friends but also do not forget to thank God for giving you such a wonderful light. You are a light to this world, who needs to share your words because they are often the last things we do; we write our wills, letters before we die and speak to our children whilst barely breathing to fill them with our light just one last time. I can remember how I felt as if my grandfathers' spirit was still with me as I watched two eagles fight it out on the day of his funeral. His light never died, and I am glad God sent me a reminder that he was still with me and yet at the same time with God. Let us choose our words, carefully alright. Be aware of what we put into this world so that no one gets hurt because of us, I have much love for words, and I do not want to see them end in violence, okay? Anyway, I know how hard it is to give my words to this world for them to judge and criticize because I know they will judge me too.

I know people will think this book about the
consequence of words is ridiculous, but it's so valuable to know
what your words can do to others. Because what words will do
is not simply enough. It's not enough to say words will do this,
and that is because the truth is, we do not know what our
words will do. We can guess and often were right, but even
Harriet Beecher Stowe did not know Abraham Lincoln would
say to her, "So you are the little lady who started this great war"
(Lincoln). The thing that Harriet Beecher Stowe did not know
is that our words outlast our lives. What we are saying now
could be heard, the next century over, no matter how long the
world lasts.

Our words do not end with our lives because it is given
so that someone will want to remember us as we were. I mean
I do not care if I am forgotten someday; I think it might be
better to not be remembered not at all. I do not want anyone
to know what kind of thoughts I was having in the middle of a
pandemic. For almost a year, I have been penning away, and
yet almost no one knows that I am a broken individual being
repaired by God piece by piece to be someone, someday. Like
this book, I am a work in progress that has yet to stand the test
of time. I do not know how the story will end and how my
words will begin the world. The truth is I want to be many
things, but I can only be one true thing, and that is faithful to
God.

As such, I want you to know I am your friend, someone who wants you to use your words for good, to value existence and live happy quiet lives filled with tons of joy brought to you by God. Writing this is the only happiness I have known for a long time, and it is a pleasure to have met you through my words. I hope you understand that throughout this mess is a person who cares about this world we live in, you won't find another one like me for sure, so I give you my ending words too. Live to love God, work to please no one and never let anyone take away your words. Live without consequence and exist to become someone worth knowing; we are all worth knowing someday. Thus, I hand over to you control of knowledge of words and consequences are now yours forever to do what you will.

CPSIA information can be obtained
at www.ICGtesting.com
Printed in the USA
BVHW010212141120
593255BV00005BA/375